YOU
FOR
YOU

FEEL AND
GROW RICH

MATT SANDY

TABLE OF CONTENTS

ACKNOWLEDGMENTS

I want to thank my university Logic and Rhetoric Professor Stephanie Brown for having written a blistering letter of recommendation for me back in the day which I found recently. Her words served as a guiding voice of reason for me to keep going:

"I can honestly say that he is one of the best students I have ever had. He writes clearly and well, managing to combine a rigorous, logical thought process with a flair for unexpected, evocative metaphors... Mr. Sandy is unusually comfortable with original thought." – Professor Stephanie Brown

Dear Reader, I hope my words will inspire you too to blow the lid off your potential and *carpe diem*.

INTRODUCTION

Think and Grow Rich was written in a time of building during the early 20th century. *You For You: Feel and Grow Rich* is written in the 21st, during an era of expansion.

My first book, *Manifesting Miracles in the Matrix: Live Your Day Like It's Your First*, emphasizes owning your energy, writing your new narrative, and taking integrated action to manifest your dream life. It is the foundation for *You For You: Feel and Grow Rich*.

One of the invisible intentions of "the matrix" is to envelop recurring language-driven programs for us to accept as true without much critical thought. Shouldn't we question why particular phrases combine words in a certain order? For example, what does it mean and why would you want to "live your day like it's your last?" This colloquialism means "not taking your time for granted" and "paying attention to the things most important to you." In order for you to do so, you are reminded of your last day on earth…wow.

Could there not be a better way to convey the underlying message? How about that, to live your life with purpose, you should release yourself from the past baggage of judgment, pain and suffering to "live your day like it's your first" for more joy, love and abundance in the present. For us to think our best, we need to feel our best.

What we strive to accomplish is always a work in progress. No matter how much we pause to celebrate inspiring wins, every day is a new day (preferably one we wish to live like our first). Our achievements are defined by our values, which may stay consistent over long periods of time. If we forget our humanity and let the dark side of "the matrix" sink in, nothing we do will matter much. What drives us to manifest is our human touch: our ability to laugh, cry, sing, dance, express our visions, and not be repressed into divisions.

You are still free to feel what you want to feel. Own that, because it is worth more than its weight in gold. You can draw your innate power from it to grow rich, to give to causes that matter most to you.

At the time of the writing of this paragraph on October 25, 2022, Triple T's brother had been "cancelled" but to the best of my knowledge T.T.T. himself had not. I listened to him speak about the term "brokie" and deduced he meant the following:

> "Brokie" is a condition of the mind. One can be poor but not be a "brokie;" while a fiscally well-off person can be a "brokie" in their mindset and subsequent behavior.

Do you wish to break free from the matrix mindset that keeps you brokie and broken?

In June of 2015, I stepped into the Tank and forty five minutes later walked out with a $600,000 offer for 25% ownership from two billionaires, one a regular and one a guest. For me it was akin to being down to a 3-2 count, 2 outs, bottom of the ninth, Game Seven of the World Series and hitting a walk-off grand slam. My emotions elevated to cloud eleven that summer. I guess you can say I sensed as close to what one can sense to feeling like a billion bucks. Nothing too crazy, simply a sensation of sunshine in my solar plexus, the external superstar validation value added to my inner state of self-worth. The deal did not go through and the episode did not air, however, which was as it was meant to be.

The matrix manifests by tethering you to external stimuli to permit you to feel good about yourself. How long can you go unplugged from the dopamine nation before needing the next hit? Can you go ahead and feel good about yourself right now on command, if you decided to do so? Look in the mirror — into your own eyes — and proclaim "I love you" to yourself. Can you do that with self-assurance? Or would it feel uncomfortable? Has the matrix cloaked you into believing that that is an act of narcissism, and muddled your mindset to disassociate you from yourself?

Today I do not need to jump through impossible hoops of hard-working accomplishments and external validation to "feel" the way I did that day in June of 2015. Lately I have also become a bit of a skeptic of anyone purporting to offer you a red, blue or any color pill in exchange for freeing your mind and/or for fiscal salvation. Be wary of cults that lead you astray from taking the reins over your own mind for independent critical thought.

Newsflash: you are your own Morpheus to your own Neo and Trinity. Preserve your power. May the essence of *You For You: Feel and Grow Rich* inspire you to believe in yourself, defeat the dogmas inside that limit your potential, and grow kinder within all realms where it matters most.

Your perception of the world is a reflection of your beliefs about yourself. If you believe you are worthy, you will courageously rise up to challenging occasions, find resourceful solutions to difficult problems, and wish to see others elicit the best in themselves. If you lack faith in yourself, you will expect to see the worst in people, be shrouded in jealousy at others' success, and sense discontent at your setbacks replaying in an infinite loop of should'ves and could'ves.

You are predestined to impact the world for the better. Socrates and Shakespeare knew well of the human temptation to turn against yourself once you reach your pinnacle of glory. Many great warriors could not handle the pressure at the top, nor the descent back down to the ground. Will you let your self-worth slip right when you need your self-love the most, to remind yourself that you matter? Or will you remember your roots and stay humble?

Winning is easy for you. Doubting your own greatness is futile because you have a true inner knowing of it. Your secure knowledge is what keeps you going, despite having wanted to throw in the towel before. The world is waiting to celebrate you– and with you – the magic you will give and create.

You do not need a litany of losses in life to learn to win big. You can raise the "abar" in your life by practicing small wins daily. Watch this pattern of behavior snowball into compounding gains:

Always Be Acting Rich (ABAR)
Feel it to Become it
Become it by Feeling it

The universe will give you more of that which you see and project forth by matching your frequency. Learn to tap into that flow of energy. Be mindful what you wish for as you can literally have any dream become reality.

The glass *is* half-full. The only time you might see it as half-empty is if wish to hold yourself back from life's limitless possibilities, and from growing a rich, resourceful pocket and mindset.

We have thusly arrived at the end of the introduction and the beginning of its conclusion. Feeling good *is* the secret: feel it to become it. Thoughts flow from emotions. Try to think and grow rich when you are not feeling like a "billion bucks" about yourself.

May you strengthen your resolve by the end of this book—your abundant "feeling" inside—to confidently venture out and make your dream life a reality. Do not wait for others to validate your innate greatness, and especially that which you already know, trust and believe is true about yourself today.

ONE

*

RIDDLECULOUS

Why do we say "I wish I'd known then what I know now?" Could it be our pain talking of losing time or resources had we only known better how to act more efficiently? Winners do not regret their decisions even if they resulted in a setback, because regret begets more regret.

The universe does not reward you for what you know or not. The universe co-creates with and gives you more of what you are and who you are striving to become at any given moment. Are you seeking to become richer in every aspect of your life? The universe listens to your energetic transmission and responds in kind. The frequency you emit registers an imprint in the universe and ricochets back to you.

The "timeline paradox" is the inherent riddle of manifesting: you are typically encouraged to manifest your dreams from your desires of today, not those of tomorrow. Not to mention, how can you possibly know what your dreams and desires of tomorrow will be? You can only know at best what you may want right now, as it is nearly impossible to ascertain the goals and desires of your future self.

If "time keeps on slippin', slippin', slippin', into the future" like the Steve Miller Band sang, would you want to "fly like an eagle" or would it not be preferable to spend your time investing in manifesting goals that will match those of your future self rather than today's self? That way you will not have spent your time in vain.

What if you spend all your time to get your "today goals" and arrive at a point in time in the future wondering why you spent all your time getting something you now do not even want or wish for? Or if you pursue your "today goals," what would happen if you do not attain them within a quick enough time window as the clock keeps on ticking? You would get stuck in the past, because your today becomes your yesterday while your tomorrow's wants outgrow your today's desires.

If you practice living in the wish fulfilled, it assumes you inhabit this wish from your "today goals." Yet tomorrow inevitably rolls around, then next week, next month and next year. The longer you hold onto what you wanted "today," the longer you will be stuck living in the "past." Riddleculous.

To compound the problem of manifesting your "today goals," you may grow frustrated over time if you do not receive what you want today quickly enough. You may even allow yourself to begin to turn on yourself, doubting yourself why your dreams are not coming true. The only "u-turn" you should be considering, though, is a "you turn" which we will be getting to soon.

Meanwhile, what would happen if you have set your intention for your dream life and you work incredibly hard towards your "today goals," but your progress is moving in the opposite direction? Yes, you put your trust in the universe, set it and forgot it, and you are doing all the steps needed. So what exactly is going on, and what is the solution?

Some experts may even profess they have discovered the secret, the one key you have been missing to open the magic door that leads to the manifestation of your desires. The problem is that the same riddle is repeated that leads you to invest time into manifesting based on the "today goals" of your present self. You will end up stuck in the past pursuing over time your "today goals" that will not match your future desires of who you will evolve to be in the future.

Where are those same experts who can tell you who you will be and what you will want in the future? They can only focus at best on who they see you as today and what you are proclaiming you want right now. Only you, and you yourself, can unlock your inner wisdom, abundance and riches to manifest today for your future self's best interests. That way you will arrive at that distant point in your future timeline proudly saying, "I am happy I know now what I did not know then."

In order to solve this riddle for yourself, you should define what your "future self" means to you. For example, is your "future self" the future you in one, five or ten years from now? With a ten-year period as opposed to one or five, things begin to appear far more distant. It is difficult to imagine what you ten years from now will dream about manifesting and what will be important to you, let alone what the world will become. Both eagles and time fly; so when that future day arrives, you will be mesmerized how time flew by so quickly.

With that in mind, imagine yourself right now as your future self, but do not project yourself today onto your future self. Answer this question to the best of your ability:

Who will you be and what will you want
in the future as your future self?

Riddleculously hard to answer.

There is no way of knowing that right now, is there? All we know today is what we have or do not have, what we wish we had today, and what action plan we will take to make it happen. How can we possibly know today who we will be or what we will want in the future? That is the crux of the riddle.

What if instead of spending days, weeks and years into manifesting what we want today — inherently causing ourselves to get stuck in the past — we focus our attention on investing our time into what our future self will be and want? This way we can invest the time it would take to accomplish our manifestation action plan to match the desires and wants of our future self at the future point in time.

Would that not be a better use of our time? Is that even possible?

The answer is yes. You can project out your future self because you know you will still be more or less human. You can therefore focus your attention on that part of your life you believe will in fact be as close to consistent as possible: your emotions. You can imagine today what you would want your future self to feel. Begin bringing into your life today that which would be in the best interests of your future self's emotional well-being.

Knowing this you can make a quantum leap in bridging the unknown by attracting and doing today more of what will enrich your future self rather than satisfying the hunger, hurt or craving of the ego self stuck in the past.

What about all the past emotional, generational and spiritual baggage you have tried to get rid of? You will have an epiphany today that there is just no more room for it on the private jet of happiness and prosperity of your future self you are about to take off in. You will put an end to tiresome old stories, butt right into your new timeline, and change the frequency of your future by espousing your own version of this vibe:

Bye bye, yesterday. Hello, today. Tomorrow, here I come.

Do you want your future self to be free of the matrix and have more joy, love and abundance than you are attracting today? Take this liberating step in this new direction of you for you. Anticipate your growth in becoming richer in mind and pocket. Act on behalf of your highest self.

Prosperity and growing richer are a function of time. You can choose to bend time by bringing into your life today that which you project will make your future self feel incredible. What you project out into the invisible quantum field is what you will receive back. Mindfully align your thoughts, beliefs, intentions and actions into one coherent movement fueled by your good feeling.

Feel and grow rich. Not so riddleculous after all.

TWO

**

MY RICH GREAT UNCLE RICH

In a recent interview, Mr. Alex Hormozi shared that rich people have varied habits: some wake up late, some early, some eat healthy, some do not. However, he posited that the rich share three traits:

1. Superiority complex: They have a bigger vision because they believe they deserve it. They think they are better than others, deserve more than everyone else, and can accomplish big goals.

2. Crippling insecurity: they feel that they will never be enough, that they "suck," and will always be measured by what they achieve.

3. Impulse control: a "beautiful mix" tying the two paradoxes together—they are able to

control their actions and focus on a single mission for a prolonged period of time.

Putting all three together you have:

- ❖ Big Goal (pulling you forward)
- ❖ Strong Fear (running away from it)
- ❖ Impulse Control (focusing on what matters)

I never saw my rich great uncle Rich dressed in anything but a suit and tie; he despised people who overslept; he loved to tell the story of meeting and discussing with the pope big world issues; and he donated his personal art collection to a museum for naming rights. He always believed he was right. Detest them all you want, but the one additional trait that is common amongst the rich is:

Self Conviction

I suppose you can say he had an air of "earned" arrogance. He was at his office every morning even up to the age of eighty, eighty-five, ninety, ninety-five years old. His eyes were always glowing like he was laying sight for the first time on shiny diamonds. He seemed to always have a gleeful smile like he had won the lotto of life…which he did.

Rich minds perceive the world differently than brokie minds. Remember: what you project out into the universe is what you get back. You can grow free of the matrix or become more attached to the matrix depending on the frequency of your vibration, coupled with your conviction. Step into that vibration of freedom, wealth and health that you desire, so that your future self thanks you later.

Every time I saw my great uncle, he would retell his story of meeting the pope and discussing with him significant world issues, as if he had never told it before. To him, it must have felt new each time. Now that I recall all those times, it did seem like he was telling this same story to himself, rather than to me. That must have been his "recalling the vibration of abundance, self-love and self-worth" story. So why was he telling it to himself in front of me?

Here he was, with everything one could dream of in life in terms of wealth, family and lifestyle. Yet he was sitting across from a much younger man whom he desperately wished in that moment he could be all over again. How bad he must have felt about himself in that moment, to the point of almost turning in on himself. But he would not bend in on himself no matter what.

He told this story because it was his happiness oxygen. To others he may have come off as conceited in doing so. That was a small price for him to pay, however, compared to the cost of forgoing his own sense of self.

I do miss him a lot. I never got a chance to share with him my books, which he would have loved.

You will often hear the phrase "the rich get richer, and the poor get poorer." This is another "brokie" phrase by its very nature, because it boxes you into limited thinking. It gives little consideration for the real ones who started off dirt-poor and built great wealth. Nor does it explain why some of the richest people in the world end up destitute. Do not get caught up in the meanderings of the matrix, as it will do everything to middleman between you and your self-conviction. The phrase should instead be: "rich minds get richer, and poor minds get poorer."

Maybe you have already experienced the "before/after" point in your life where you were finally pressed to stand up for yourself from a place of love, not fear. You heard the calling loud and clear from within: "your time is now." Was it your voice speaking or was it a voice from above? You are not sure, but what is certain is that your "feeling" about yourself took a massive turn. You cannot remember anymore the days you used to see the cup half-empty, dreading existence in its entirety.

Maybe your "self-feeling" changed because you found your purpose doing what you are passionate about. You cannot quite put your finger on it, but you are conscious that you added awareness into the equation, shedding light onto embracing your imperfections and those of others, too. You realized there is no time to criticize, only time to realize what you fantasize. Your mindset grew rich, and your feelings grew richer. Your dreams no longer sounded downright crazy to you, but rather actionable roadmaps for upright reality.

It stopped mattering as much as it did in the past what others think, because you grew to love yourself enough to trust your intuition. Making mistakes no longer meant you were a mistake. You began experiencing the electricity of evolution. You started learning and doing better next time, every time. Your connection to your inner self gained impenetrability as a beacon of light and love, for both you and for the outside world.

You stopped comparing yourself to others and even to yourself. Your values and what you stood for started to matter. Your goals emerged embedded and imbued with strong faith, serving a higher purpose. You chose to let go of the helplessness that was not helping you inspire yourself, and others to aspire to a high threshold of excellence in thought and action. The self-sabotage days were now so long gone it was as if everything happened by design for you to find the strength you never knew, but always suspected, you had within.

You took a "you turn."

THREE

***

YOUR "YOU TURN"

You will always vividly remember "that day" in your life. It is the day you begin to recognize what many believe but science cannot prove: the existence of a higher power. It may be the day you hit rock bottom and make the decision to quit quitting; knowing with certainty that now it is only up from here, no matter what.

You will become focused on a big goal, believing with a renewed sense of confidence you can and will achieve it. The chances will be high that you will gas out or lose sight of this goal because various pressures, distractions and obstacles will be thrown your way: the universe tests you before it blesses you. You will persevere, knowing nobody can take from you what you earned and now truly own:

Your Faith

When you awaken to the epiphany that you can turn this belief onto yourself, that is the day you make your "You Turn."

Turning your faith onto yourself, you will witness the truth that was there all along, no matter how much someone or something did not want you to see or feel it:

You Are Worthy

You Are Abundant

You Are Magic

Your actions will no longer simply be movements towards self-centered, ego-driven "goals in life." They will become coherent, cohesive co-creators with the universe in your mission of mindfulness, expansion of consciousness, and enlightenment.

Strengthen your inner faith towards yourself daily. Grow to trust that you are worthy without being overtaken by the giant you may inevitably become within. It is a delicate balancing act.

Even if you feel you get n
towards your goals on the tc
still practice empowering
world. Impress upon the ¹
make positive change in yoι
environment and extern
universe will always receive and respond to your
energetic transmission when it is intentionally pure.
The matrix, on the other hand, will do everything in
its power to make you feel unworthy of your
connection to your higher self.

Match your affirmations with strong feeling and
faith. For you to affect powerful change in your life,
you must step into the feeling what you anticipate
will be most ideal for your future self. Do not get
confused by terms such as "present" and "future,"
thinking they are two separate beings. You are one
and the same: a human "be-ing" living to "be" your
"best" self—with an extra "a" for "abundance" to
"be" your abundance-attracting "be_a_st" self.

Your future self is you here in the present
manifesting the feeling you wish to inhabit to attract
more of that which you want. Merging timelines to
the realm of "no time" lets you enter the divine state
of neutrality to connect to your powerful energy.

rs in "faith" are comprised of clues for
-leaping to your peak performance:

❖ Frequency: match the energetic frequency
  of vibration of your intended outcome.

❖ Attitude: the attitude of gratitude — be
  grateful for all, positive and negative.

❖ Integration: integrate mind, body, spirit
  and emotion in one alignment to feel and
  have certainty in your outcome.

❖ Trust: let go and trust, believing in a higher
  power and that the universe is working
  with and for you.

❖ Happiness: this one may take time to
  master, but will be at the counterintuitive
  core of your success — you must be happy
  now without any precondition, externality
  or doing anything special, knowing you
  already are special and complete.

Recall an event where you were victorious, proud and joyful. Ask yourself:

- ❖ Were you in the **frequency** and energy of your successful outcome?
- ❖ Were you naturally embodying an **attitude** of gratitude in the moment?
- ❖ Did you feel an **integration** between being internally aligned and certain you were going to succeed?
- ❖ Did you practice non-attachment and **trust** that the outcome was going to happen like you intended and visualized?
- ❖ Were you **happy**, regardless of the outcome, knowing all is as it should be?

You had faith. You believed in yourself. You knew it was possible. As you relive that event now, imagine that the universe is working today to align for you all the right circumstances for your next victory. For the universe to get it right for you, it needs you to be clear, concise and consistent. Stay focused, grounded and intentional.

Great things are coming your way. Be wary of the trix of the matrix.

FOUR

****

TRIX OF THE MATRIX

The matrix distracts you, whereas the universe attracts you. The matrix does not want you to know yourself, while the universe awaits you to connect to your higher self.

The matrix programs and intercepts your thoughts from thinking and growing rich. The universe wants you to awaken to see that nobody should get between you and your energy—that within you is your roadmap to growth.

The matrix wants you to believe that weakness is strength so it can allure you with distractions. The universe gives you more of who you are—which is painful to experience when you are weak—bestowing abundance on strong energies.

When you go astray of the matrix, it cajoles you back with a bag of tricks. When you go astray of the universe, it creates arduous experiences for you to grow stronger in order to enhance your force within needed to manifest what you have always wanted.

If you are not here for you, who are you here for?

Everything in the universe is a projection of your energy, frequency and vibration, of which your feelings and emotions are at the center. What you set your attention on—along your inner belief in it, expectation of receiving it, and vibration of self-worth—is what the universe will send you more of.

Strong thought flows from strong will. Weak thought follows weak will. A strong will is the feeling inside that you earn by taking risks and overcoming challenging situations.

If you want to think strong thoughts and grow rich, you must first feel yourself already abundant, so that your thoughts flow from the strength of already having that which you want.

What do you believe is the answer to the following question:

What does "rich" mean to you?

The simulation of the matrix thrives on fundamental human feelings of unworthiness and doubt. It fills them for you with a mirage and a barrage of tricks. Sometimes you are left momentarily satisfied, while other times you are left completely mystified.

Meanwhile, the universe waits for you to awaken to the awareness that you have the power of your own perception. Choose what you want to expect to receive more of, and focus your attention on this with commitment, consistency and clarity.

"Rich" is a matter of your own perception. If you define rich as having a luxury home, an exotic car collection, a private jet and an expensive lifestyle, you may not allow yourself to truly "feel rich" unless you have those things. As result, you may pay even more attention to those who flash these possessions. This in turn will remind you more of that which you do not have and that which you wish you had. How will that make you feel?

The matrix does not want you to know the irony of it all. To begin to attract the lifestyle you believe defines "rich," you should start to feel rich today — right now. How?

For you to "feel rich," you can change your definition of what it means to "be rich." Imagine if you can perceive "being rich" as being grateful for light, air, water, trees, and your pulse. If you are truly happy with and in gratitude for all you have already as you move towards your goals with strong intention, you will enter the vibration of "being rich." The universe will in turn send more opportunities for wealth and prosperity to you. The matrix does not want you to know this.

You will then feel the strength of your own self-abundance that will begin to attract that life for yourself you thought was unattainable from your previous definition of "rich."

The epiphany will be all yours:

Your Self Worth is Your Net Worth

You may have heard that your "network is your net worth" and that we are the "average of the five people we spend the most time with." However, that is only partially the case. Imagine you are the richest person in your area code. The five people you may spend the most time with may be nowhere as rich as you. That does not make you less rich. What ultimately limits you is your own idea of what it means to be rich, how to live up to your own expectation of it, and whether you feel that you are abundant already to continue to attract more of that.

You will only be and become as rich as you limit your own self-image and self-worth to be. If you ask for a million then that is what you will be capped at because you did not value your self-worth as a billion dollar brand. This is one more thing that the matrix does not want you to know. It wants to get between you and yourself so that you no longer believe what you have is good enough to feel rich.

As you begin to "feel and grow rich," your definition and perception of rich will evolve beyond what you used to make it out to be. Recall the manifesting riddle? To quantum leap beyond it, manifest today what will be in the best interest of your future self's well being—rather than filling the lack of your "today goals" that will expire over time.

Catch yourself if you get upset paying attention to what someone else has, does, or what someone else's life is. Do not become swayed by that. This is another seductive trick of the matrix:

Comparison is the Thief of Joy

The matrix thrives when you are upset because it distracts you from your inner wealth within. Nothing makes the matrix happier than keeping you scatter minded and flustered from your own awakening that you are abundant right now.

There are endless tricks of the matrix meant to deter you from your own power within, including tantalizing you with illusions. If you are at wit's end thinking what is it all about and how can you win when all the odds are stacked against you, your response should not be to "give up" or to "not want" anything. If you do that then you let the matrix win by default. It will then fill your lack of willpower and lack of sense of self by feeding you mindless solutions for that lack of self determination.

The goal is to become free of the matrix. To do that, you need to want what is right for you. Not what the matrix gets you to believe and limits you into thinking is right for you.

The matrix is so insidious, invisible and impermeable that the people closest to you might even be afflicted by its power. They may be its unwilling subjects broadcasting to you its values that are completely contradictory to what is in your best interest. They may be your closest loved ones but it does not mean they know what is best for you.

This becomes especially true the more successful you become. Everybody will want to be your friend to give you support and advice that they purport is best for you. They will claim to be "looking out for you," have your best intentions at heart, and to not want to see you go astray or get hurt. Their stated desire to only want the "best for you" does not mean they do not wish positive outcomes for you. However, success should only be defined for you by yourself—not by others' definition of it for you.

Be aware. Only you know what is best for yourself. Maintain that inner knowing at all costs.

Go ahead now and give this question your attention. Answer it to the best of your ability:

Who is the richest person in the universe?

Take all the time you need to reply to this question from your best and highest self. Imagine now you are talking directly to the universe and putting forth your dreams. The universe is checking—are you in the vibration of self belief, self-worth and self abundance of that which you seek? Have you given this question some thought?

The only right answer should be: you are.

You are the richest person in the universe right now. You are reading this seeking to grow more abundant in all ways possible. You are already in the vibration—feeling state—of being rich. Right now, right this second, you are tuned in, concentrated, and focused on your goal.

Bob Dylan sang "the times they are a-changin".

As we enter the Age of Aquarius, more people than ever are coming offline the matrix and online to the universe. The times changed.

Now is the time for the song to be updated to "the people they are a-changin". We are seeing the light and love all around, and attracting more of that abundance in with pure intention.

So...who is the most valuable person—MVP—in the universe?

You are.

Correct answer.

You are on a roll.

FIVE

*****

MVP – MOST VALUABLE PERSON

I originally subtitled this book *Become a Billion Dollar Brand* which sounded like mission impossible. In fact, it is mission possible. It has been done by others, so it can be done by you, for you.

Here are three reasons why you may want to set your sights on becoming a billion dollar brand:

1. In the first film, Dr. Evil in Austin Powers sets his sights on one million dollars. In the second, we see his self-worth evolve as he says "why make trillions when we can make… billions?" What you ask for is a reflection of your inner self-worth.

2. If it sounds unattainable, perhaps you should consider it as you may grow and discover more about yourself the bigger you dream.

3. Combining one and two together: if in the end you do not attain the goal of a one billion dollar brand, and fall short at say 999 million…well that's 999 million more reasons to celebrate. So no matter where you fall short of reaching this goal, you will have a lot of reasons to celebrate your success.

What does the term "billion dollar brand" mean? When most people think of billionaires or a billion dollars, this level of success is off the charts. It is desirable to attain if one could or knew how to do it.

We can suppose the reason it is attractive to attain is not only due to the financial freedom it affords but also the ability to perform philanthropic acts to make a positive impact on the world. Achieving this goal would facilitate the realization of one's innate desire to give back to heartfelt humanitarian causes.

There are only a few people in the world that have attained this level of wealth and prosperity. In fact, it is so rare that approximately twice as many people climbed Mt. Everest. However, achieving it does not mean that it can be held onto forever.

The famous saying goes that the first generation builds it; the second generation preserves the wealth having witnessed the hard work that went into creating it; and the third generation, never having experienced the work for the creation of it, lets the wealth go to waste.

What is a "billion dollar brand?" In September 2022, MrBeast turned down a $1 billion offer for his YouTube channel. This is the literal meaning of a "billion dollar brand." MrBeast is paving the way for a new generation of content creators. It is your time now to create your wealth.

A "billion dollar brand" is also a metaphor for your "be_a_st" self. The world may exhibit various vibrations of negativity. That does not mean you have to go along with that. Nor does it mean you have to define your identity around it. You always have the power of choice. Will you react or will you act? Remember when you chose to act like a conscious, aware and empowered human "be-ing"? You decided you are going to be your "be_a_st" self — your "best" self with an extra "a" for abundance.

Each one of us comes into this world fully abundant, complete and perfect the way we are. It can take a whole lifetime or faster to discover that.

Becoming a billionaire brand should not feel like it is out of reach if one is willing to put the work and discipline in. It is ultimately about whether you trust yourself enough to know that you are always moving in the direction of being your be_a_st self.

What is the foundation of a "billion dollar brand?" One word: Value. Be the MVP—the most valuable person.

Start by being an MVP to yourself—always honor yourself. Allow yourself to be in tune with your intuition. That is your key to your incredible treasure within that makes you unique. Be in touch with what you are most passionate about. Even if you only have a few extra minutes a day, plant the seeds of your beautiful garden with that which you love to create. It will blossom because pure love is the language of energy, frequency and vibration. The more you value your creation, the more expensive it will become to acquire that which you have built.

How do you create value? Labor, luck and love.

SIX

******

LABOR, LUCK AND LOVE

Whether you currently labor at what you love, or do not love where you labor, you always have a choice to act or to react to the circumstances. Always bring your best attitude. The universe is watching out for your best self while the matrix thrives when you get upset if you do not enjoy what you are doing. You should always be laboring with love to create a landing spot for luck. What is "luck" and how do you do that?

By now you should already expect that we may be questioning the cliché explanation that "luck is when preparation meets opportunity." This phrase has been attributed to Roman philosopher Seneca (though there is little evidence that he said that).

Imagine you just finished your meal, pop open the fortune cookie, and the phrase inside reads "today is your lucky day — a great fortune is coming your way." You check your lotto ticket and see you have the winning numbers. Who is luckier in this instance: the creator of the fortune cookie message or you the winner of the jackpot?

After all, that same fortune cookie message was opened by many others but they never won the lotto at the same time like you did. The odds of opening that specific message and winning the lotto at the same time is much smaller than you simply getting the winning ticket. How many messages did the creator of the fortune cookie make previously that never got opened by someone that won the lotto at the same time? The creator of the fortune cookie message is luckier than you in this instance because they had overcame greater odds than you for such an improbable event. But you, with less luck, got a bigger reward.

Luck is therefore "getting disproportionately rewarded for being at the right place, right time." It is thereby the easiest thing in the world to get rich — once it happens. You can simply chalk it up to getting lucky. Many try to work hard in the matrix to create opportunities to match their preparation, going round in circles believing they have control over outcomes and seeking their date with destiny.

Once you realize that you have no say in luck — it just happens — you can let go of expectations or disappointments. You can also begin to attract luck into your life in its purest vibration frequency energetic essence. Bruce Lee's message is to be flexible and malleable: "become water my friend." My message is "become luck my friend." How? Ask for it, meditate on it, and do it carefully from a rich mindset that already has all the luck in the world.

However, do not expect all the problems to be solved in life when you put the effort in and make a windfall. Money reflects more of the true nature of the real person inside. Always know what the "disproportionate reward" is that you are asking for from the universe. Be in the movement of perpetually raising your own ABAR: "Always Be Acting Rich."

Keep moving forward and be sure to ask the universe: "what is needed now to continue to act from the energy of wealth, health, happiness and prosperity?" The matrix does not want you to do this but the universe will respond to your request.

A perfect example of this going wrong is the reason that the aforementioned third generation loses the wealth built by the first. One theory is that instead of valuing the "wealth creation energy" that was necessary to build it, the third generation thinks that type of energetic existence is too stressful. It is foregone as they now have all the material wealth they need. They want to enjoy their life to the fullest and believe they know the secret that you also now know: "luck" is a major factor for attracting an intended outcome. However, the third generation misunderstands the power of luck pretending to have a superior understanding of it now that they live off the hard work of the previous generations. So they ask the universe the one thing they know they can get because if the first generation got rich, they know they can also get what they want now: "how to enjoy life by doing nothing stressful, and getting rewarded disproportionately for that?"

This request is a rare instance when both the matrix and universe align, albeit for different reasons. The matrix is on permanent stand-by mode ready with all the expensive experiences and fancy toys, bells and whistles. The universe meanwhile reflects back more of the energetic equivalent.

In this instance: nothing stressful. The third generation goes back to nothing because that is what they wanted. They disproportionately valued "nothing stressful" over the value of what they already had. The irony is they end up more stressed with nothing than had they worked to maintain what they received as did the second generation.

Be the MVP of yourself and of your generation. You will bring greater good to the world and change the luck for the better for others. How will you create and maintain your landing spot for labor, luck and love? Focus. Well, actually a bit of magical hocus focus.

"Success is the ability to go from failure to failure without losing your enthusiasm"

– Winston Churchill

SEVEN

****

HOCUS FOCUS

It is difficult to focus if you do not feel good about yourself. To think and grow rich, you first need to feel really good about yourself in order to then think the right thoughts. How can you be a great gardener otherwise? How can you pull out the weeds of negativity if you do not feel good enough about yourself to put the effort in for building great wealth inside and out?

Luckily the universe handed you on a silver platter a great gift: the power of "neuroplasticity." This gives you the ability to change and to grow rich based on what you focus on. In a way, you are like the proverbial "third generation" that has been bestowed with great wealth and abundance. The previous generations overcame impossible odds and toiled to build the systems, organizations and structures in place to grow rich.

Think of the things we did not have a hundred years ago. Humanity needed to "think" all the time because it was constantly in building and wealth creation mode. It took extraordinary thought to discover Moore's Law that the number of transistors on micro processing chips doubles every couple of years. That is just the tip of the iceberg.

Today many people profess to be experts with an opinion on any given subject matter. The ones that thrive and become super rich exhibit high EQ (emotional quotient) and a solid sense of self-worth: they are aware what others experience and are able to feel rich inside without preconditions.

Master your emotions to make your inner sensei proud. Develop empathy, listen, learn and lead. People will follow your inspired leadership to make the world a better place.

The world will call it magic. Practitioners will call it technique. You can call it hocus focus because you perfected surfing your mind's hypnotic waves.

Alpha Waves: the most valuable brainwaves for peak performance. When you are fully engaged with your subject matter while calm and relaxed at the same time, you are allowing yourself to be in the alpha frequency of 8 to 12Hz. You are more creative and can absorb new information with ease, entering a sort of hypnotic work flow state of concentration. It feels magical to lose track of time as your stress is reduced while your productivity levels increase. You feel good about yourself in the alpha flow state.

Theta Waves: the portal between your dream and waking state that occurs in the frequency of 4 to 8Hz. This is the time you become drowsy before falling asleep at night and upon waking up in the morning. Negative thoughts are least prone to thwart your affirmations from acceptance by your subconscious during this time. Theta is the optimal frequency to access your subconscious to reprogram patterns with hypnotic auto-suggestion phrases. It is also an ideal time to feel good by experiencing internally inhabiting your intended outcome.

Enhancing the power of your alpha and theta waves contributes exponentially to your focus. You can take the necessary steps to do so. What are these steps to take to maximize their potential?

Activating Alpha

The first step to unlocking more of the alpha wave hypnotic productive flow state frequency is to create real rewards that are deeper and longer lasting than chasing fleeting hocus pocus pleasures. The matrix loves to interject here between you and yourself with the advice to "do what you love." That type of directive can leave us more lost than found. What to do? Focus your intentional energy on those activities that make you feel good about yourself that are well thought out in advance by you.

Always be acting rich about your environment: creating a clean, quiet environment with a simple, well organized desk is crucial to reach your hyper focus alpha flow state. Minimize the distractions that can derail you from your state of concentration. Press go when your energy level is normally high, blocking it off in your calendar as deep work time.

Love the game: the orchestra is ready to play upon seeing the conductor vivaciously lift the wand. Create your own original cue to train your brain to access your alpha flow state. If you do exactly the same ritual every time before starting your work, your mind will recognize it over time and enter the alpha state faster on your command.

46

<u>P</u>ure joy: reflect on the rewards that life has to offer often. Set clear objectives by getting excited and writing down the rewards you will gain from your actions. Reduce the difficulty of the goals and rewards by making them plausible. Break them down into the smallest possible daily habits.

<u>H</u>ave a plan: sharpen your focus to pay full attention to a single task for a short period of time such as fifteen minutes. Increase the time you are able to singularly focus on the task until you are able to stay present and concentrated in the moment giving it your full attention for longer time periods.

<u>A</u>wareness of risk: you can fail without winning, but you cannot win without failing. Trust the process and absorb the power of resistance. When you overcome resistance, you absorb its power as the greater the resistance, the greater the power. You will start to see these pockets of discomfort as power-ups in the game.

One of the bonus outcomes is that you will learn what you find most meaningful and do more of that. Give yourself the time you need for yourself to implement the positive practices over time to become a positive habit in your daily regimen.

Thankful in Theta

You will uncover a deeper connection to your inner voice and values. You will acquire clarity on what motivates and incentivizes you to be your best self. You will fuel your good feeling about yourself.

Time to self actualize: solidify your gains as you drift off to sleep at night by way of self activating affirmations and repeating autosuggestions such as "great wealth is coming my way."

Harness your growth: repetition is the key to making the power of neuroplasticity work for you. Repeat your statements slowly, quietly and lovingly when accessing your subconscious in theta.

Expect good things: how you feel determines your thoughts and what your subconscious reacts to. Dwell on already having love, peace, health and abundance as if you already have it in the present.

The work is done: let go of the past. The degree you are able to "let go" is the degree you are able to "let in" what you actually want to receive. Practice having a feeling of serene certainty that all will be solved by the universe in the purity of your request.

Awaken to a new you: be aware as you awaken in the morning that you may hear an internal voice and receive an answer to your request which may be fleeting as you emerge out of theta. Keep a notebook such as your *My Dream Life Story* guided journal to write it down first thing in the morning. Repeat once more your affirmations in gratitude.

As you transition out of theta, tie it all together by empowering your expectation of good things coming your way in the day with the phrase:

Show me how good it gets today

For this to be effective, you must already feel good about yourself and believe it is possible to do so. The intent of this phrase is to honor and celebrate yourself and your ability to tap into your own good feeling that you are now producing internally without the need for external stimuli.

You begin to open up to the realm of infinite possibilities. You may even smile ear to ear as people look at you funny on the coffee line on a gloomy morning pouring cats and dogs outside. They may wonder either you won the lotto or are high on potenuse.

You have discovered the feeling of gratigood. You are full of gratitude and feeling good.

EIGHT

****

GRATIGOOD

The "right feeling" unlocks the "right sequence of events." You cannot retroactively create the "right feeling" by way of thoughts, beliefs or externalities. That would only create a feeling dependent on and justified by those thoughts, beliefs and externalities.

Keeping a gratitude journal will make you feel good conditionally as you train yourself to feel good for that which you are writing gratitude for. You may not feel good in totality. Your goal is to feel good in totality from within your own inner power source regardless of externalities.

Your internal "good feeling" should be your own internal sun, planets and universe inside you radiating love, joy and abundance no matter what is going on in the outside world. No matter what your mind may be thinking or how your body may be acting, "feeling good" is the engine that unlocks everything. It has to be a pure, unencumbered state.

From this state of "feeling good" you can unlock the beliefs about yourself to blow the roof off your sense of self-worth without going overboard. You can unlock that state of self belief about yourself that you did not have before when you thought you were not worthy.

Now you feel that you are worthy and more worthy than you ever thought before. You reach a new level of worthiness within where now you are ready for the greater abundance level than you previously thought you deserved.

Worthiness is a state of belief. When you have the good feeling that is working for you that unlocks the beliefs that you want, then you can manifest with good intent the best scenarios for your future self.

The matrix will please your desire to feel good by sending your way the environment, externalities, circumstances, and practices—especially positive practices that you are told to. It will do this so your desire to feel good is temporarily met. Or even worse, it will intertwine your good feeling state to be dependant on those externalities. Once those externalities are removed, you will no longer feel that good feeling you had before.

The universe on the other hand wants you to discover by trial and tribulation your true inner power within. This is the power to practice and retain your "good feeling" no matter what. Feeling the "good feeling" *is* the secret — not thinking or doing or acting in a certain way to feel some way that is fleeting. Feel the purity of the "good feeling" from within yourself from nothing but from within your own self. This "good feeling" is the feeling of:

Gratigood: "gratitude" plus "feeling good"

To achieve the "gratigood" feeling you can go beyond the limited programming of the matrix to access your own highest self as long as you are aware you are initially relying on the assistance of this method. Practice it enough times to remain with the "gratigood" feeling in its purest form after having removed this method's assistance.

"Gratigood" Method

Take a moment to meditate on and recall one of the best times or events in your life when you were happy, celebrated, and feeling really good with gratitude for everything and everyone. Believe you are in that state of being right now and hold that state for several minutes. To avert the tricks of the matrix enveloping your first person frame of perception, speak directly to your own universe ("youniverse") from that state in the third person:

"Why are you working so hard in life to feel this way again? Why can't you feel this way right now even if you are not getting in life what you want right now? What if you allowed yourself to go there and sense that greatness within that is always there within you? How would that feel to feel really good about yourself like you did that day right now?"

You will know when you have that strong good feeling within for yourself. Once you have practiced this enough times you will remain with your good feeling in its purest form. It is your purest inner energy that flows from the same source from which all life is created. You are the youniverse.

NINE

****

YOUNIVERSE

What you tell yourself is what you will receive. This is because you and the universe are co-creators in the intended outcome of your desires. Begin to expect good things and the universe will send you good things. Begin to see the cup half full and the universe will send you more to fill your cup. Begin to feel "gratigood" and the universe will seek to match your energy by sending you more situations, circumstances and opportunities matching your energetic equivalent vibration frequency.

The energy you put into what you wish for is what you will get regardless if you say you want it or do not want it. Sometimes that which you do not want happens faster than that which you wish for.

Why is it that when you do
something it sometimes happens fast
you wish for something you actually do
is happening is that even though you do   .ɔɩɩ to
have it, you are actually applying your attention to
the desire of not wanting it. The matrix loves it when
you do that because it lets the universe do the work.
The universe matches your energetic equivalent
frequency and gives you more of that which you do
not want because that is where your energy flows.

You have read *Manifesting Miracles in the Matrix*,
applying it by writing your narrative in your *My
Dream Life Story* guided journal. You arrived at this
chapter by way of already knowing that:

You are Your Narrative

Write and update your narrative often. Why?
Doing so trains your mind to seek out the clues and
signs you need to hydrate and energize your
abundant feeling for sustained and positive growth.

Living in today's world we are max matrix
overloaded. Every day our minds are exposed to
tens of thousands of visual, auditory, and sensory

a points. What is absolutely unbelievable is that our minds absorb everything — even though we may think we are blocking out what we do not want. Every thing! Our minds see every detail without us being consciously aware of it.

Writing and updating your narrative is an exercise of tuning your mind to focus on that which you want and wish to embody. Want to manifest miracles? Become the universe to yourself.

Feed your mind with visual, auditory, and sensory data of that which you want – from within! Not by watching, hearing and experiencing what you want from the outside – but by creating it from the inside out. Match it with "gratigood."

Your mind has the power of two-in-one for you: it has the capability of both a giant movie theater and a billboard. See yourself realizing your dreams on the big screen in your mind and see your name in lights. You are a billion dollar brand – right on!

Take five minutes for yourself at night before falling asleep and visualize in the big movie theater of your mind yourself living in your dream home. Imagine with specific detail the design, layout and location in full vibrant color. Add to it the sounds you would hear and feel the emotions you would experience in this billionaire's palace. See, hear and experience your own personal journey you will have taken to achieve this in your new reality.

Imagine you are replaying it in your mind as if you are right there, in the moment, with full certainty, in the present. Most importantly, experience the feeling of worthiness—you made this happen out of your highest self intentions of love and abundance. You did this because you wanted to give back to the world, make a positive impact, and make it a better place for the future.

Set the intention to yourself: "I will write in *My Dream Life Story* guided journal in the morning, and include my day's plan, top three non-negotiables and give gratitude." Promise yourself you will take guided and intentional action with forward loving energy. You have the power within yourself to self discipline, do the work that becomes easy work once you get going, and maintain the intention to yourself to give it your best shot.

Remember: do not make failure out to be a bad thing. Why? The word "failure" traces back to the

Latin *fallere*, which meant "to trip" – since tripping is a mistake. When we make a mistake, we learn from it and get stronger. Do not associate your identity with any mistake. If you are giving it your best shot, you will get stronger and ultimately succeed.

To raise your percentage of success against your overall attempts, you should keep improving your performance and increasing your shots on goal. Implement regularly the one-two punch of "listen and light" — we will get to that.

Regularly write your dream story narrative with specific details of your intended dream life. Your billion dollar actions come from a place of courage, philanthropy and positive impact. The roots of that can be traced to your good self feeling.

Success is a function of where you imagine and clearly see yourself being — and the degree to which you can do so with a high level of belief — multiplied by your quantity and quality of shots on goal. Review this formula for success as it will be your measuring stick for whether you are keeping up on all fronts for your be*a*st self.

Success Formula:

$$\{ S = xB \times cI \times P \}$$

S = success
x = degree of belief $\{1...\infty\}$
B = belief
c = degree of clarity $\{1...10\}$
I = image
P = performance/productivity

Becoming a billion dollar brand is an intended wish outcome event. You may be reading this book for enjoyment and only flirting with the idea of it. Or you may be reading this book and quite serious about this goal. In either event, reaching any goal, no matter how conceivable or inconceivable, requires you to increase the degree of your belief in that reality, along with increasing the clarity of your own image of achieving that in the power of your performance and productivity.

Perhaps you have resigned to the fact that you will never be a billion dollar brand. But if you can earn a million dollars you will have enough money saved up to afford the life of financial freedom. That is perfectly amazing to have as an intended outcome. In this case, for you the term "billion dollar brand" would mean achieving a state in life where you are free to pursue what you want to do, on your own calendar, in pursuit of your own happiness and vision for a beautiful world.

Therefore, it is always important for us in setting our goals to be careful and clear what we truly want to accomplish so that we do not loosely toss terms around. As we grow and evolve in multitude of ways, it is important to be mindful.

TEN

****

MINDFUL

This is a beautiful word because the mind is full of untold riches and capability to change the world for the better. What would we be if we did not stop and think in moments that required us to rise up to the occasion and be our best selves? Right now we are collectively living through some of the most turbulent times in history. And yet somehow, life goes on—and on and on and on and on and on and on and on.

To be mindful is to observe and label thoughts, feelings, and sensations in the body in an objective manner. Practicing mindfulness brings greater peace helping to become more relaxed. This allows a pathway to our internal selves to effect change.

Why is this important? Between having to choose between becoming a mindful billion dollar brand vs. an unmindful billion dollar brand, we would most likely wish to choose the former, not the latter. Why would we wish for a mindful outcome?

We have the power to ask for whatever we wish for in our internal reality. It is mindful to be specific upfront and classify our intended outcome to bring more peace, joy and abundance rather than one that will lead to more pain and suffering.

There are always thought vampires that lurk in the shadows. Believe you me, they will be first to come out in full force of vengeance once you attain your billion dollar brand goal. Their energetic pull is oftentimes so strong over one's will that it causes good people to lose sight of the ideals they once cherished and held dear.

This is the allure of having so much. With great power comes great responsibility. This all starts with your ability to be mindful of what you ask for, and what the reality will be once you achieve it. The sooner you start practicing "listen and light" the more ready you will be to counter once you achieve your goal and push comes to shove.

Mindful living is placing your faith in the recognition that we are all flawed beings. Nobody is perfect. We are all under renovation, constantly improving. That is the beauty of it. Figuring it out is part of the divine dance. Wouldn't it be more fun to figure it out with other people who love life and celebrate all the best it has to offer like you? There is so much more to becoming a billion dollar brand than just the numerical achievement.

It is about recognizing that you are worthy for whatever it is you set your mind to achieve. The only person that matters in accomplishing your goal is the one inside your head. You should expect the world around you to think you have absolutely lost your marbles if you claim you are going to become a billion dollar brand. That is a given and as long as you are aware of that you know you still do not have your screws loose.

Life is not about other people's opinions of what you can or cannot do. Do not compare yourself to anyone else — including to your own self. It can be hard not to do so with comparison cues around every corner. This is where you draw a line in the sand. Are you in it to win it? Are you committed?

You For You?

Give me a "F Yes". Good.

Recognize the beauty in this awareness:

Your Imperfections Make You
Perfect the Way You Are

It may very well be that which you least like about yourself is in fact what will end up being "the" thing that generates the power and mission for your billion dollar brand. No kidding.

I was bullied in middle school and wished many times with twenty-twenty hindsight I would have acted differently in response. I simply did not understand with my childhood awareness at the time that I was not sensing I was being threatened. This was because I could not gauge the concept of bullying. Why would anyone have it in them to want to belittle another person?

I came into this world a super happy kid always smiling thinking the rest of the world was the same. It was not easy to wrap my consciousness around the alternate reality.

I decided the fault had to be mine and that something was wrong with me. Wow, talk about the exact opposite conclusion you would want your kid to arrive to under the same circumstances.

For me at least, my lesson from the universe was being delivered quite early. I was being guided repeatedly to recognize a core truth of human endeavor and character that I simply kept overlooking and taking for granted:

You For You

At the end of the day, nobody is going to stand up for you and fight for you better that you can for yourself. The moment you let your inner demons get the better of you, you resign to an opposite fate to that which you intended for yourself.

Losing is ok. Getting your ass kicked really sucks. Failure is fine. Giving up is not. Get back up no matter what. Give it another shot. Even if you are hurt, or bleeding, "get to the choppa." Never, ever give up on yourself. Whatever you do, never ever lose faith in yourself with regards to any part of yourself that you may loathe or be ungrateful for.

You are given a set of clues at the start of the game. You have it within you to put the pieces of your puzzle together in such a way that it fits into a beautiful story of abundance distinctly for you that you achieve in a completely unique way unlike anyone before or after you. The universe will always test you before it blesses you because it wants the be**a**st in you to come out and play.

Be mindful. Manifest your dreams. Be specific about what you want, and especially the why of it all. Why do you want it? How will it make you feel? Why do you want to feel that way?

Are you running away from a past hurt, or are you running towards an incredible new direction of joy, abundance and connection to greatest consciousness of the universe? For every answer you give to your why, ask why again.

Why are you doing this? What is it you truly want? What is it you were divinely sent here to do? To give? To create? To share? To unlock for others? To contribute? To build your legacy on?

You may have heard this somewhere before but it is worth repeating like fine wine or a good song:

What you tell yourself is what you will receive.

You and the universe — "youniverse" — are co-creators in the intended outcome of your desires.

Expect good things and the universe will send you good things. See the cup half full and the universe will send you more to fill your cup. Feel "gratigood" and the universe will seek to match your energy by sending you more situations, circumstances and opportunities matching the energetic equivalent of your vibration frequency.

Begin to believe in yourself and your power to create a forest of money trees, and it will be so.

ELEVEN

****

MONEY FOREST

Wow, you made it this far! Congratulations. Your commitment to yourself is impressive. You are taking action acting on your intuition. I am grateful we have this time together in this amazing journey. Let's go!

We are told many things about money. There is one interesting rule that starts with this supposition:

Money does not grow on trees…

Have you heard this saying before? It basically means do not spend your money on useless things because you will not get it back. Spend it on things of value that will bring your life more abundance and prosperity. Education, self-growth, family — invest in things of value that will compound more value to enhance yourself, your outlook, career, friendships, relationships, know-how, etc.

With that in mind, the expanded rule is:

Money does not grow on trees...
Unless you are the Money Forest:
Become the Money Forest.

Go forest go.

Are you committed enough? Becoming a literal meaning of a "billion dollar brand" is not about a 999 million dollar brand or 998 million dollar brand. It is about becoming a billion dollar or higher brand. Get furious. You are going to need all the energy you can muster within yourself to cross the finish line. Get angry at yourself for not having gotten there yet. Now let that anger go. You do not need to live in the vibration of anger but you can utilize anger to jumpstart your motivation to accelerate your high profit action taking.

So let's talk about you and me, let's talk about subjects baby.

Specifically, the subjects of knowledge you are going to need to master to "become the money forest" and subsequently, a billion dollar brand.

Firstly, what is a money forest? Many money trees grow and thrive in your money forest. It is abundant, positive, inspiring and marvelous forest comprised of incredibly valuable, gigantic well rooted trees full of big green leaves of plentiful money. So much money is growing on these trees that they can fund anything, anytime, anywhere. Philanthropy? Yes.

Perhaps you are may start to get triggered by all this money talk. The voices may creep up from the shadows. This is good. This is what you want. Let them come out.

You want to hear what these voices are saying to you from the inside. You need to hear this self talk and absorb its power for your own good intentions.

Do not be afraid of the matrix negative self talk vampires that seek to thwart your beautiful goals. They do not like the talk of money because they thrive in reminding you of their limited beliefs such as "money is the root of all evil." But guess what?

You have the power of light. Let them say all they want to you. You are going to smile and deliver the one-two punch combo of:

"LISTEN & LIGHT"

BOOM. KO.

One: you are going to jab with your lead hand by listening and writing down what they are saying. You need to hear all the negative self talk because you are going to take your pen and paper and write it all down. To rewrite your narrative from within to empower your money forest, you want to become a master gardener and uproot the weeds that reside within. To do that you need to know where the weeds grow, what they are saying to pollute your forest, and how to invert their negativity to plant seeds of positivity in your forest for new money saplings to grow into big, strong trees.

Two: you are going to deliver a hard blow by lighting these suckers up. These negative thought vampires suck your energy, time and money from your goal of prosperity, health and love. What do vampires fear the most? Light. So go for it.

Courageously hold that light up to them of love, abundance and happiness and witness them flee the scene like the cowards they are. Just because they somehow got into your forest does not mean they belong there.

Healing and maintaining your forest is the first step to building a forest full of plentiful money trees. Choosing love over fear, you can, and will, let go of the emotional baggage holding you down. Your goal is too important now to be weighed down by phantoms and fantasies of negativity and fear.

You can, and you will, invert and absorb the power of their punches for your abundant and courageous movement forward towards your goal. Your motto now is: You for You.

That's right. You are here to fight for yourself, not against yourself. You are here to love yourself in all your glory because from within is the abundance from which you will invent, build, grow and successfully maintain your money forest.

Why do you want it? Is it the FleurBurger 5000?

TWELVE

****

FLEURBURGER 5000

"Why" is the most powerful and therapeutic question we can ask ourselves in letting go of past hurt in order to heal and attract into our lives exactly that will make us only happier. Why do you want to become a billion dollar brand? Is it about proving something to yourself or to others?

Who are you doing it for? Why? When you start asking yourself why three times, you begin to take back the power to yourself recognizing what it is that you want most out of life. As part of writing your dream life story, ask yourself regularly: Why, Why, Why?

We are by nature highly emotional creatures. Even the most rationale of types may belie deep, unmet emotions of love and connection driving them to become even more analytical rather than opening up creative channels of consciousness.

We do not like to be wrong. So we cling to the lies that we know to be true. We fall in love with our own triggers. They give us the reasons we crave to feel significant. If the outside world is not giving us the significance we deserve, we can surely rely on our triggers to give our ego a much needed boost. It is difficult to let go of the pain from the past—if we do that, what life raft of identity would we have left to cling on to?

On the one hand you need to develop a high emotional quotient (EQ). On the other, you have to learn what is going on inside your own consciousness. Today's environment is aggressively dopamine dumping and sapping your serotonin from every angle. That challenge is a lot to ask for. Where to even start?

You may actually be growing faster today than you have ever before. You simply do not know that is happening, let alone are able to recognize it. It may feel to you like you are losing confidence.

In fact, what may be going on is that you are

changing your form and shape to take on new challenges that you otherwise would never have contemplated in the past. It is all happening so rapidly that you have little time to stop and see it happening in real time.

That which you least value within yourself may be in fact the most valuable. The only way you could discover that is by raising your awareness of your own thoughts, decisions and behavior.

For example, if you are repeating the same mistake, chances are you are not alone and others have similar habits as well. It could lead to a new idea for a product invention that the market will appraise at a significant value.

Develop a keen eye for the most common problem you face every day in your life. Does a solution exist for it already? Or is it something that no one has solved the way you would? If you decided to solve it, what would you do differently?

Money is an exchange of value. You can get paid for the same service two different prices by two different parties depending on the value they ascribe to your service. Automate and scale your service to be able to solve the problem for many parties at the same time globally around the clock. Be unique in the personalization and care of your service so it is a level beyond that of the competition.

It all starts with why. As you understand yourself better, you will begin to seek out and see improved results and outcomes in your personal and professional pursuits. Your ability to find creative solutions to difficult problems will begin to come naturally to you as you embrace more complex and highly nuanced situations.

Too many good people have achieved their financial goals to self-sabotage their extraordinary accomplishments once they have arrived at their destination. Why does this happen? They will work so incredibly hard, finally getting to the peak, only to wonder "is this it"? Their inner voice may go off: "so now that I am a billion dollar brand, is this what it feels like?"

Like what? What does it feel like? Why did they wait all that time to get to the pinnacle to discover what it felt like? Are *you* going to make the same mistake? F No.

Do not wait to discover what it feels like to get where you want really want to go when you can feel that today. You can expedite discovering where you really want to go by asking why, why, why.

There is no time in life to await the gratitude and happiness you can feel today, right now. Take this moment to pause, and do this exercise:

Take a deep breath in, pause two seconds, say with your chest voice "Mm-hhmm", then breath out and say with your throat voice "Ah-Ha!"

Do this three times while affirming with your internal voice "You are a billion dollar brand."

It may take a few tries to get the hang of it. What this exercise does is combine several key tenets in one effective approach to grounding yourself in your new reality. It merges breath work, feeling and inner voice affirmations into one electro-magnetic force to powerfully influence the invisible quantum field around you—the field that surrounds and connects us all. Meditate on it mindfully.

How do you feel after doing that? Do you feel stress? Do you feel any type of anxiety or fear that you are not worthy of that? That is the clue to you to release the energy blocks you have within that hold you back from inviting more love, light and abundance into your heart space. Have no doubt that you are absolutely worthy of it, if not more.

If ten people reading this right now do this exercise, it will positively change the vibration of at least one hundred people in the world (if each of the ten cares for an average of ten people in their life). Imagine if 100 people are doing this exercise collectively. Wow! If 1,000? Incredible. 10,000? We, together, can change the quantum field for the better of millions of people by doing this exercise united in a stadium to affirm our new reality of releasing ourselves from the pain of the past and stepping into the amazing presents of the present.

Own your now. Yes, that is the name of my book *Own Your Now*. It is a quick, very densely packed short read that will guide your compass internally to attract from within the abundance that is already within you. Owning your now means that you have elevated beyond reacting emotionally to lower vibration emotions that have tethered you to a linear time scale preventing you from taking off like a rocket to achieve your goals. You have come in tune with your highest self to recognize that energy in the universe cannot be created or destroyed — it can only be transferred or transformed. You have learned how to do exactly that, transforming yourself to the superhero with a divinely gifted treasure map within you for your own unique path and discovery.

Expounding on that, a key step forward for your success will be to actually thank, forgive and absorb the power of those people that have wronged you in your past. Let them go from harming you right now. Just because they harmed you in the past does not mean they are harming you now. You can absorb the power they took from you back and multiply it.

People will right you, and people will wrong you. But will you wrong yourself? This is not a rhetorical question. There is only one right answer: F No.

Correct. Winner, winner FleurBurger 5000 dinner.

FLEUR BURGER $5000: 100% Wagyu beef, Hudson Valley Foie Gras, Truffle and served with a bottle of 1995 Chateau Petrus at Fleur Las Vegas.

To clarify, an F Yes to the FleurBurger 5000, and an F Yes to doing right by yourself. Never has anyone achieved anything great without a good amount of self belief.

So what are the steps to success? This is where the path gets interesting. If anyone were to publish a book claiming to be a step-by-step manual for becoming a billion dollar brand, you would have to take extreme caution in following it as it may very well lead you off a cliff. The reason for that is someone else's steps to success cannot be replicated by another human being. This is due to the law of time and timing:

> Law of Time and Timing: Each person is subject to their own timeline and the timing of their actions in so far as it has matched their successful intended outcome.

In other words, you absolutely cannot achieve another person's success. You can only achieve your own success due to the law of time and timing as applied to you. What you *can* do is expedite your own timeline and improve your own timing. While we would like to simplify things down to numerical values, such as comparing one billionaire to another billionaire, the truth is no two success stories are alike. The only similarity may be the supposed net worth of the money forests.

How they grew their forest is their unique story. It may or may not work for you. At the end of the day, when you end up growing your money forest, will you really want to be like someone else?

F No. Correct. You are going to want to be recognized for your individuality and what made your success story unique and inspiring for others. Now that you are a billion dollar brand — how did you make it happen? Do you feel more secure than ever about yourself or do you still feel unworthy?

Remember the "crippling insecurity" that is common amongst those that become rich where they feel that they are no good and will never be enough? What the matrix wants you to believe is that feeling unworthy is a deep inner pain you should run away from at all costs. It has all the answers for you with titillating distractions, contraptions and attractions. The universe, on the other hand, wants you to discover that if you can actually feel unworthy then you are alive. You have the power within to convert your pain into purpose, and self quantum skyrocket.

81

THIRTEEN

****

SELF QUANTUM SKYROCKET

Why don't we feel worthy? Is it because we are inundated with images of perfection, unattainable fortunes and the uber successful broadcasting what an unbelievable lifestyle they lead — that we too can it for the nice price of 9.99, 99.99, 999.99, 9,999.99 and so on? That is a lot of 9s like the Beatles sang.

That can make us feel unworthy and is exactly what the matrix wants. The irony is that the universe wants you to be able to feel it as well, but for a completely different reason of self empowerment. Are you ready to self quantum skyrocket? F Yes.

First, do not confuse "feeling unworthy" with "feeling good" about yourself. When we "feel good" about ourselves, believe it or not, we may also still be "feeling unworthy." Again, we must get very clear on the meaning of this sensation we experience in mind and body that we call "feeling unworthy." What is it at its core?

"Feeling unworthy" is a phantom pain we experience when we let someone else's perception of happiness to matter to us and judge ourselves for not having that which we believe we should. We develop an internal sensation of pain for not having that which we believe we need. The matrix is on standby to "help" us fill the internal lack. The only perception that should matter is yours.

"Feeling unworthy" is our mind processing a great deal of information that we then try to make sense of consciously to cross-analyze with all the data we are receiving. What do we naturally do with data when we analyze it in our minds? We compare it, contrast it, organize it, add it up, and calculate the score of what we think it means.

For example, we go too far with it using sports metaphors to rate others and describe sensitive human experiences together. In other words, we let our minds run completely amok. This is exactly the type of entrapment the matrix wants because it sidetracks you from your source energy and leads you down a path in which you end up "feeling unworthy." You end up feeling not "good enough" because you allowed someone else's projection to get you to believe they are better than you so you should be like them.

Let's get something straight here.

Are you a 10 in intelligence? You are an 11.

Are you a 10 in personality? You are an 11.

Are you a 10 inside and out? You are an 11.

To clarify, F Yes 10 to all but because you are off the charts the regular numbers do not apply to you.

Next time you start comparing yourself to others, or others do it to you, see the letters "DNA" pop up on your mental screen:

Does Not Apply & btw my boss DNA is off the charts

You see how good that feels? Maybe you cannot completely shake off feeling unworthy. That is ok because what matters is that you are allowing yourself to feel really good about yourself. You are using the power of neuroplasticity to make the most important choice you can about yourself — you for you — rejoicing in your "gratigood" internally.

Do not let the matrix get between you and yourself and distance you from your abundant billion dollar brand called yourself. Yet if the matrix wants you to feel unworthy, why does the universe also want you to feel unworthy? Our goal should be to feel really good about ourselves and it feels really bad to feel unworthy. So what is going on?

You may get into situations in life where you may feel conflicted about having to make a decision between two options and paralyzed with fear about making the wrong call. There is no right or wrong choice as it is based off your perception.

We have a tendency to chase the experiences in life that we think will make us feel good, while trying to avoid the experiences that we think might make us feel bad. The reason the universe wants you to experience the sensation of feeling unworthy is because it wants you to make the only choice that you truly need to make: you for you.

Once you choose yourself, you begin to unlock with intentional forward moving energy the gifts that you never may have thought possible before. Magical doors open up to you to allow you to fill the world with more love, light and abundance that you already have inside yourself.

When we do not feel okay internally — "feel unworthy" — we may opt for the tools and tricks of the matrix to convince ourselves that the moments we experience have to be a certain way in order for us to feel okay, or not to feel worse. The problem is that we think that in order to feel good, something needs to happen or not happen. For example, it needs to be a sunny day or it should not rain.

The universe wants us to understand that "feeling unworthy" is like the experience of internal rain. It is simply an experience: we can choose to run out to dance and soak in it, or open up an umbrella and avoid getting wet.

Depending on what you decide to do is your highway to self quantum skyrocketing to the moon when you choose you for you to feel and grow rich.

Amazingly, each one of us *is* the interface to both the external universe and our own internal universe of thoughts, feelings and beliefs. Our interface also comes with a sort of an energetic radio transmission tower whose signal to the universe we control the amplitude of to make our dream world become real.

FOURTEEN

DREAM WORLD INTERFACE

We can simultaneously exist in the matrix and the universe. The matrix was created to be a lightning fast program to analyze and categorize the flux of the universe into numbers and sequences. This is a net positive as the universe utilizes the matrix to co-create your dream world with you into reality.

How badly do you want what you seek? The universe will do a quality control check before matching the vibration of the experience you are creating in your interface. If you affirm "I want so badly to be a millionaire," the universe will check the strength of that desire and match that vibration by sending you more experiences for you to "want so badly to be a millionaire."

If instead of that you are affirming, "I am grateful to be a philanthropic billionaire brand," the universe will check the power of your belief—specifically if there is any resistance in you in that belief. If you feel worthy of it, the universe will do one of two things. First it will cross check with the network of the matrix to see if you already have that which you claim. Then it will either send your "ticket" to the matrix to send you a test—it plans to bless you but checks to ensure your intent is true with no doubt—or it will proceed directly to create the opportunities and circumstances for you to receive in reality that which you already believe you have.

In other words, your dream world creates the imprint on the matrix. The universe then fills the gap if the energetic transmission you send out is pure.

You can experience the wealth, abundance and prosperity of feeling and growing rich right now. Believe it is already here for you now because you can vividly see, taste, hear, smell and touch it in your dream world. Shifting your self image about yourself, you can upgrade your expectation from "I hope everything works out" to "what if everything works out?" This shifts your entire expected experience of your divine dream world interface.

All life is created from the image of the divine based on pure, perfect laws of behavior at the corresponding scales of existence. Life is happening simultaneously on many scales, from the too-small-to-see nanoscale of atoms and molecules — so small that a single nanometer is one-billionth of one meter (seen only by electron microscopes) — to the unfathomably enormous intergalactic scale (for which the James Webb telescope is deployed).

Patterns and structures may be recognizable to us that repeat similarly across scales. Or they may function mysteriously to our understanding such as the spooky Quantum Entanglement theory that won the Nobel Prize in October 2022.

You are the interface that has access to your internal universe capable of creating a dream world which you can then transmit out to the external universe. What can you do with your dream world?

You can dwell on the positive, or you can wallow in the negative. We can get stuck in the negative when we associate the tattoos of trauma as our fault. Or we can release ourselves from self judgment by forgiving and absorbing the power of those that have wronged us in the past. Being harmed then does not mean you are being harmed now.

You are free to choose. To solve the "manifesting riddle" think what you can do today so that your future self will thank you later with your investment of time, work and effort. To self quantum skyrocket, choose consciously the best experience for you.

How you experience life is key to which mirror you will reflect from the external universe and what gets amplified your way from the outside. For example, what if you imagined going through life thinking "what if it all works out for me?" What if the emotional setback, heartbreak, or pain you may be dealing with is simply a point on your life map preparing you for or connecting you to something amazing? Take it a step further and begin to expect good things to happen. Make it a habit. Be specific.

This cannot be emphasized enough: when you are seeking to manifest a new job, a new car, a new home, a new relationship, a new life, anything at all—be very clear about it. Are you coming from a place where you "want it so badly" to fill a void? Or are you coming from a place where you feel real "gratigood" about yourself and the outside world?

Your dream world is your gateway to manifesting your ideal reality. Regularly write and update your *My Dream Life Story* guided journal with detail.

The practice of writing and regularly holding yourself accountable in your *My Dream Life Story* journal will accomplish two important things that you have already anticipated based on the understanding of the dream world interface:

1. Internal: It focus the power of your neuroplasticity to create new intentions for your inner world—mind, body, spirit and emotion—to be aligned to what you pay attention to. This alignment empowers your electro-magnetic signal to be clear and coherent in the invisible quantum field transmitting a strong frequency to the energetic signature received by the universe.

2. External: You begin to see and experience life differently as you start to come from a place of believing you have and are worthy of that which you want. You understand that the moment you ask, it has already been created for you. You change your destiny with that which you wish for—your dreams—which already exist as electromagnetic potentials in the quantum field of the universe.

To get anything you want—wealth, joy, love—harmonize your "wishing tree."

FIFTEEN

****

WISHING TREE

We arrive on our journey to one of the most important trees in your money forest — the "wishing tree." If there is one chapter, one top takeaway from reading this the first time that you can save, it is to dwell on and absorb the significance of your own "wishing tree" and what it means.

In order for you to realize your dream world in the real world, you must be aware of the internal energy road blocks that prevent you from getting there and the external matrix obstacles that will allure you to seductive detours along the way. Are you going to be stoic enough?

You must feel worthy of that which you want and assume you already have in the present. Recall the "superiority complex" of the rich: they have a bigger vision because they feel they deserve it and think they are better than others to accomplish big goals. In short, they not only think they are enough, but they go a step further and believe they are more than enough to bring their dream world to reality.

The universe and your highest self cannot distinguish between a million or a billion. They are one and the same to the universe which will always match you without fault to your energy vibration equivalent. If you believe you are worthy of only a million dollars instead of a billion, what works is the strength of your attraction vibration which is based on the strength of your conviction.

Your Self Worth Limits Your Net Worth

Having a lower self-worth leads to having a lower net worth and prevents you from believing in yourself and claiming what is yours. You must get to the bottom of *why you do not feel worthy* to bring into reality your real deal dreams and realize abundance.

All thought comes from the mind. Your goal should be to shift and transform your mind into a "wishing tree." Your mind may be scattered putting out proverbial fires moment to moment. Or it could be oscillating, one moment moving in one direction, another moment going a totally different way.

The goal is to make it pointed in one direction consciously and consistently with conviction and without conflict. The key is the consciousness and awareness of the power of your interface – to decide on how you act or react to life's internal and external experiences.

When we speak of the mind, you are its driver. Once you develop this awareness, you become a conscious being that has the keys to your kingdom. Now comes the part of alignment in one direction.

This is where the "wishing tree" comes in. In a well organized consciousness with a strong mind, whatever you ask will become reality. To develop this strength, the alignment of your four pillars of mind, body, emotion and spirit is paramount. Specifically, if you think one thought, but your body moves in another direction, and you then feel a third way, but you believe something different, you will be out of alignment of your "wishing tree" potential.

For you to develop your "wishing tree" to an elite level, you must become aware of the thoughts in your mind, the care of your body, the sensations of your emotions and the foundation of your beliefs. Harmonizing all four areas into one, unified forward moving direction is what will provide your "wishing tree" the power to manifest anything you want.

Feeling good about yourself expedites your ability to do that. Feeling bad about yourself blocks your energy from making it possible. If you really want what you are seeking, you will stop all the habits that are holding you back and become committed to your own self excellence above and beyond all the voices, distractions and obstacles in your way. There is no room for wrong when you are being right for yourself.

This is why the "wishing tree" is one of the most important trees in your money forest. From this tree any dream, vision, desire will become a reality for you. You will be able to imbue your goals and embody your wishes with the invisible force of the universe known as "intent". This is the force that shamans have known that provides infinite strength for mere mortals to carry out superhuman feats. Couple your "wishing tree" with "intent" and look out! You are feeling and grow rich by the minute.

Practice conscious self care.

SIXTEEN

****

CONSCIOUS SELF CARE

You are becoming stronger for yourself by the minute. You are committed to improving your life, becoming a better version of yourself, and sharing with the world your highest self. You need a plan of action to materialize your big dreams. Fear and pain always arrive ready to push us back from our goals. A conscious self care plan helps offset setbacks, and should be built on a foundation of:

❖ Knowing and meeting your needs

❖ Nurturing and treating yourself kindly

❖ Recognizing you are deserving of self-love

❖ Feeling good about yourself, flaws and all

❖ Rejoicing in the power of self belief

Every day you show up for yourself is a day that makes the universe smile. The more you make the universe happy, the more aspiring your results will be in reality. To accomplish that faster you can remove that which you want less of in your life. You do not have to feel good all of the time if you are reducing the energy allotted to those things that make you feel less than good about yourself. You can allow yourself to reflect on the bad days, and why things are not going the way they should. Doing so is a lot easier the more you prune from your path those habits and situations that you wish to experience less of after confirming they are not conducive to your highest self.

Saying no can be more powerful than saying yes. Be reflective and conscious of what you want less of in your life. Make a commitment to align your time and energy to your values. You may be spreading yourself thin trying to please others with plans on those days that you would rather rest and focus in the free time for yourself. It is not selfish to practice healthy self care. As you align your "wishing tree" to perform at its best, begin to practice physical, emotional, spiritual, mindful and social self care.

Physically:

- ❖ Are you getting enough sleep?
- ❖ Is your diet healthy?
- ❖ Are you exercising regularly?
- ❖ Are you drinking enough water daily?

Emotionally:

- ❖ Do you express your feelings freely?
- ❖ Do pet peeves get under your skin often?
- ❖ Do certain emotions tend to bottle up?
- ❖ Do you repeat relationship patterns?

Spiritually:

- ❖ Do you make time you need for yourself?
- ❖ Do you believe in a higher power?
- ❖ Do you ask questions about life?
- ❖ Do you engage in fulfilling practices?

Mindfulness:

- ❖ Are you taking care of your mental health?
- ❖ Do you practice self-compassion?
- ❖ Is your inner dialogue kind to yourself?
- ❖ Are you learning that which you enjoy?

Social:

- ❖ Are your social needs being met?
- ❖ Are you nurturing family and friendships?

Every day that you proverbially come into the office for yourself is a day that you are moving in the direction of your best self. That is what the universe wants to see and that is what we will free you of the matrix. Make it a habit to treat yourself like the CEO of yourself — Chief Empathy Officer.

It has been a true pleasure to be a guide on this journey for you. I hope this book has helped inspire you to see that all is possible when you begin to approach yourself with more love and kindness. You are a miracle that was manifested in the universe and have the power to manifest any miracle you set your mind to.

If you have not already done so, give yourself a high five and share this book with yourself again in a few weeks time. Come back to it often as it will remind you that despite all the turbulent times, you have the power to choose how to act in a conscientious forward self loving manner. May we continue to grow our community of kindness, love, light and abundance as we enlighten the world with the new way of attracting abundance.

You for you — feel and grow rich. Good luck, you already have it — the journey begins on page 99 ☺

ABOUT MATT SANDY

Matt Sandy is the inquisitive best selling author of *Manifesting Miracles in the Matrix*, *My Dream Life Story* and *Own Your Now* which have inspired many to recognize and realize their highest self. His purpose is to inspire and motivate individuals to harness their inner greatness and quantum potential.

BY MATT SANDY

Acquire the knowledge for Manifesting Miracles in the Matrix to bring into reality that which you strongly desire and implement it with the guided journal My Dream Life Story.

www.mattsandy.com

Made in the USA
Middletown, DE
11 March 2023